SAZANKA
Refined Teppanyaki Cuisine

Refined Teppanyaki Cuisine

SAZANKA

Text: Rodney Bolt, Masashi Nonaka, Kasia Cwiertka

Photography: Stephane Verheye & Olivier Chenoix

stichting
kunstboek

Foreword

There's always a touch of Russian roulette about eating at a teppanyaki table. Who is going to come and sit down beside you around the grill? Those two bottle-blondes, perhaps? Patsy from Ab Fab look-alikes, trying to send texts on their mobiles while simultaneously tackling their food with chopsticks. Or that Russian businessman celebrating the fact that he's just notched up another 23 properties to his name? Or you might suddenly be sitting beside the Dutch celebrity, who has seriously been applying himself to the task of sake tasting, and sails up to the table three sheets to the wind, to regale all with surprising anecdotes from stage and movie world.

But under the inspired guidance of master-chef Nonaka, Teppanyaki Restaurant Sazanka does not hold such colourful table experiences in store. After a genteel greeting, your private teppan chef guarantees a good atmosphere at your grill plate, and lets you in on the skills of his culinary art. No twirling peppermills here, à la Japanese State Circus, flying about to every nook and cranny of the room before the merest morsel arrives on your plate. Just inspiration, passion, and care for the product.

My first teppanyaki experience was at Sazanka. It came way too late, because I had thought that if you wanted teppanyaki you had to be on your knees the whole evening, at a table that was just a bit too low, with a geisha at your side bending double in a tight dress to pour your sake and serve you. And that each time she did so, you felt like saying: "Duckie! Watch your back!"

Instead, the dishes served up were mouth-watering, surprising and pure in taste. Like the pheasant dish that so often adorned the specials menu. A pheasant prepared and presented in a delicate Japanese way, rather than smothered in sauerkraut, as you so often get it in Holland. And the secrets of the art of slicing were always an intrigue — one that seemed impossible to transport back to a home kitchen. We are hugely looking forward to the recipes set out in this book. We'll be sharpening our knives, and trying to toss our peppermills in the air, catching them after just one twirl. And the sake won't be in the microwave, but warming slowly in a bain-marie.

I bow low to chef Nonaka, and we in the Netherlands can consider ourselves lucky that he has chosen to base himself here to cook.

With thanks,
Paul de Leeuw, Professional Amuser / Amateur Cook

Each of the recipes in this book serves 4 people.
The following measures are used: 1 teaspoon = 5 ml / 1 tablespoon = 15 ml

The Curious History of Teppanyaki

The word *teppanyaki* means 'grilled on a griddle'. In a teppanyaki restaurant, you sit at a table rather like a bar counter, around a large metal hotplate. Chefs prepare food directly on this griddle, with the guests as spectators. All sorts of menu variations are possible, but the basic format comprises a starter of tiger prawns, grilled in front of you, and a main course of steak with fried rice. Everything is richly seasoned with soy sauce, and comes with all the allure of the Japanese culinary tradition. In most teppanyaki restaurants, there is a complete absence of raw fish, seaweed, fermented soya-bean paste, and all the other ingredients that once frightened off people not used to Japanese cooking. But there is no real mystery in this, for teppanyaki was specifically developed for Western palates.

Although teppanyaki has spread through thousands of restaurants worldwide as a Japanese style of cooking, people in Japan see it as Western cuisine. Most teppanyaki restaurants in Japan have Western interiors, and cooks stylishly got up in Western chefs' toques. Their training is in a Western rather than a Japanese tradition. There is no argument about it — fried steak is still very much a Western, not a Japanese, dish.

Beef became a citizen of the Japanese culinary world barely a hundred years ago. The emperor officially lifted a taboo on the eating of beef in 1872, but it wasn't until a few decades later that the government began to promote the production and consumption of beef, in a drive to improve public health. Up till then soya products, rice and other grains, vegetables, seaweed and fish were the chief components of the Japanese diet — although game was also eaten in some regions. Many foods that commonly graced Western tables — such as beef, dairy products and bread — were barely known in Japan. Western culinary thought at the time viewed a diet without meat and milk as unhealthy. This opinion was reinforced by the fact that

Westerners were seen as generally larger in physique and more robust than Japanese people. As Japan began to modernize, the government decided that the introduction of Western foodstuffs might lead to a strengthening of the country's military and economic might. In 1869, the authorities set up the Cattle Company, a venture aimed at coordinating the production and consumption of beef and milk in Japan. The new policy laid the foundations for the development of what we now call wagyu beef, which is today renowned throughout the world. But wagyū, like teppanyaki, is a product of twentieth-century innovation, and not — as is so often supposed — the result of hundreds of years of tradition.

The origin of teppanyaki goes back some sixty years, and is closely bound up with the occupation of Japan by US-led Allied forces after the Second World War. Its invention is officially ascribed to one Fujioka Shigetsugu , the owner of an eatery named Misono, in Kobe. Before the war, Fujioka had run a café, but as a result of post-war food shortages he decided to convert it into an *okonomiyaki* diner — a move many of his colleagues were making at the time. *Okonomiyaki* is a sort of wheat-meal pancake with finely cut vegetables. These days, all manner of other ingredients are added, such as egg and shellfish, but in wartime even the sauce that was sprinkled on top was a luxury. *Okonomiyaki* means 'fry what you like', but in reality that more often came to mean 'fry what you have'.

In those hard times, *okonomiyaki* was good value not only because of the affordable ingredients (rice was completely unobtainable), but because it was cooked directly on an iron griddle. Not using a pan was one way to save costly fuel. It was to just such a restaurant that Fujioka converted his café, running it with some success after 1945 in the city centre. Dancing-girls from a nearby nightclub were regular clients, and they brought American soldiers along with them.

After Japan surrendered, the country was occupied for nearly seven years. From 1945 to 1952, more than 400.000 mainly American soldiers were stationed in every corner of the land. And the occupying soldiers — just as they do everywhere in the world — fraternized with the local women. The soldiers were decidedly unimpressed by the floury pancakes. To satisfy their tastes, Fujioka cooked the odd piece of black-market beef on his griddle. That was a decided success. For the soldiers, who had been living for months on a mess diet of tinned or frozen meat, it was a feast. Misono was such a hit that by 1952 Fujioka had put aside enough money to completely renovate the ramshackle eatery. He began to experiment by cooking shellfish and vegetables on the griddle, gradually inclining a little more towards local palates. In 1960 he opened a second restaurant, in the centre of Tokyo. That one became frequented by the business and artistic elite of the city, and Fujioka's successful formula gathered imitators.

Japanese guidebooks from the 1960s list teppanyaki restaurants as a 'new trend'. They were classified under Western cuisine, not Japanese. In the course of time, teppanyaki became less the realm of the elite in Japan, but its Western character remained. During the course of the twentieth century, all manner of foreign dishes and ingredients came to be very much at home in Japanese kitchens — yet teppanyaki was still seen as exotic, a foreign style of cooking. The Japanese are amazed at the curious position teppanyaki has outside of Japan — as one of the most representative styles of Japanese cuisine.

Although Fujioka is undoubtedly the innovator behind grilling meat on a *okonomiyaki* griddle, he was not responsible for the success of teppanyaki in the West. That honour goes to the owner of the Benihana restaurant chain, Aoki Hiroaki — commonly known by his Americanised name, Rocky Aoki. He is the man who put teppanyaki into its 'traditional Japanese' jacket, and made it a trend worldwide.

Rocky arrived in New York in 1959 — an ambitious 20-year-old with big dreams. In 1964 he opened his first little restaurant in Manhattan, specializing in teppanyaki. He constructed the restaurant (and all Benihanas that have sprung up in the ensuing decades) in the style of a rustic Japanese tavern, giving guests the impression that the cuisine was also one of the treasures of a centuries-old Japanese tradition.

To this day, the Aoki family is still the power behind a successful chain of nearly one hundred restaurants, mainly in the US. Benihana restaurants can also be found in capital cities across the world, from London to Lima, Moscow to Dubai and Istanbul. The influence the Aoki family has had on trends in international cuisine is intensified by the fact that thousands of others have imitated their successful formula.

The chief reason for Rocky Aoki's success is that he had a good feel for what the American dining public wanted — familiar food, in an exotic, exciting surrounding. A Benihana menu comprises American favourites, such as steak, chicken, prawns and a few vegetables. The excitement comes in the cooking itself. Rocky is the man who came up with the juggling of knives and peppermills at the teppan griddle — in what has come to be called 'spectacle cooking'.

In the Netherlands, the first teppanyaki tables appeared in the 1970s — in the Hotel Okura's Yamazato restaurant. This followed a trend in top-class hotels in Japan, where teppanyaki restaurants had been introduced to cater for guests who wanted an exotic dining experience, but who did not really appreciate Japanese cuisine. In 1978, the

Okura opened Teppanyaki Restaurant Sazanka — specializing entirely in teppanyaki.

From the 1980s onwards, a number of mainly Chinese restaurants began to take on the Benihana formula. The phenomenon spread, and today you can find teppanyaki restaurants in almost every major town in the Netherlands. Alongside sushi, teppanyaki has become the style of cuisine most readily associated in the Dutch mind with the culinary culture of Japan. That, as we now know, is a very curious state of affairs indeed.

Adapted from an article by Katarzyna J. Cwiertka, which originally appeared in Bouillon! *magazine*

Grilled oysters with beef soboro

- 8 oysters(Gillardeau no. 2) {1
- 160 g minced beef {2

> **For the *soboro* mix**
- 8 g sugar
- 1 teaspoon soy sauce
- 1 teaspoon sake
- 4 g hot pepper paste

> **For the sauce**
- 80 ml *dashi*
- ½ teaspoon soy sauce
- 2 teaspoons oyster sauce
- ½ teaspoon sugar
- ½ teaspoon sesame oil
- 6 g *katakuriko* (potato starch)
- 6 ml water

- 1 small onion (24 g) {3
- a few shreds of dried chilli
  peppers {4
- salt and pepper

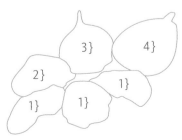

before you start

Cut the onion into thin slices. Soak the slices in water for 30 minutes, then drain and dry on a kitchen towel. Open the oysters carefully with an oyster knife and wash the shells.

tip

Don't cook the oysters for too long, or they will lose their flavour and structure.

WINE: Soft red wine, light (no or soft tannins), red and black berries.
EXAMPLE: Cabernet Franc Saumur-Champigny, 'Lisagate', Vatan, Loire, France.

method

1 To make the sauce, combine the *dashi*, soy sauce, oyster sauce and sugar in a small saucepan and bring to the boil over high heat. Dissolve the *katakuriko* in the water. Remove the sauce from the heat, and thicken it by slowly adding the dissolved *katakuriko*, stirring constantly. Allow it to simmer for a further 5 minutes, then stir in the sesame oil. Put aside and keep warm.

2 To make the beef *soboro*, lightly grease a skillet and place it on high heat until sizzling [1]. Fry the minced beef for 2 minutes, tossing constantly and seasoning with salt and pepper. Add the sugar, soy sauce, sake and hot pepper paste, and bring to the boil, stirring constantly.

When all the liquid has evaporated [2], add the warm sauce [3]. Mix through, and keep warm.

3 Place the oysters shell-side up on a lightly greased teppan griddle at high heat [4], squirt a little water under the shells and steam them very quickly (for about 30 seconds). Remove the shells and set aside.

4 Cut the oysters in 2, turn and cook a little longer, then remove them from heat and replace them in their shells.

5 Place a thin slice of onion on each oyster [5], spoon some beef over the top [6], and decorate with filaments of chilli pepper [7].

Scallops and green asparagus with ravigote sauce

- 4 scallops {1
- 4 green asparagus tips {2
- 20 g rucola (rocket) {3
- 60 g Little Gem lettuce {4

- 2 teaspoons long black wild rice

> **For the ravigote sauce**
- 75 ml olive oil
- 30 ml apple cider vinegar
- 1 teaspoon white wine
- 18 g banana shallots
- 2 g salt
- pinch of white pepper

tip

Be careful not to cook the scallops for too long. They need only the briefest moment on the teppan griddle.

WINE: White, fresh soft peach-style fruit, medium acidity, light mineral bite in the dry final tastes.
EXAMPLE: Pinot Gris, Comtes d'Eguisheim, L. Beyer, Eguisheim, Alsace, France.

method

1 To make the ravigote sauce, first mix the salt, apple cider vinegar and white wine. Add the finely chopped shallots, white pepper and olive oil, and blend well.

2 Fry the wild rice [1] on the teppan griddle in a small pool of oil at a high heat, until the grains puff up and turn crispy [2]. Add a touch of salt and set to one side.

3 Shred, wash and drain the lettuce. Wash and drain the rucola. Pile the lettuce and rucola in four scallop shells [3].

4 Cook the scallops very briefly on a film of oil on the teppan griddle — about a minute each side, at medium heat. At the same time, grill the asparagus tips very lightly on a separate part of the teppan griddle [4].

5 Place the scallops on the salad in the shells, decorate them with asparagus tips, and then pour on the ravigote sauce [5]. Finally, add the fried wild rice.

Salmon tataki

- 240 g sashimi-quality salmon (edible raw) {1
- 10 g salmon roe {2
- 4 spring onions {3
- 1 *eringii* mushroom {4
- 20 g *wasabi* {5
- leek, finely shredded

> For the sauce

- 25 ml soy sauce
- 50 ml rice vinegar
- 50 g sugar
- 5 g *katakuriko* (potato starch)
- 5 ml water

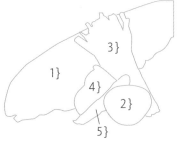

before you start

Make the dipping sauce early, as it requires refrigeration (see method).

tip

It is easier to cut the salmon cleanly if you sear it briefly on each side.

WINE: Crisp acidity, slightly salty dry aftertaste.
EXAMPLE: Albariño, Dona Rosa, Rias Baixas, Spain.

method

1 To make the dipping sauce, mix the soy sauce, rice vinegar and sugar in a small pot and bring to the boil. Dissolve the *katakuriko* in the water. Remove the sauce from the heat, and slowly add the *katakuriko* mixture, stirring all the time. Simmer for a further few minutes to thicken. Allow the sauce to cool, and then refrigerate it.

2 Remove the lower part of the salmon fillet (near the lower fins) and discard. Cut the remaining fillet lengthways into 3 equal pieces. Then cut the pieces across, into rectangular parallelepipeds (parallelogram-shaped cuboids), about 4 cm x 4 cm x 8 cm. Wipe the teppan griddle with oil and sear the fish at high heat for just a second or 2 on each side [1], then plunge it into a bowl of iced water [2]. When the salmon has cooled,

take it out and pat dry with kitchen paper. Slice it in thin pieces (less than 1 cm wide) with a sharp knife [3].

3 Blanch the spring onions by dropping them into boiling, salted water for about a minute [4], then immerse them in cold water and allow to cool. Squeeze them a little to remove excess water, then cut into lengths of 4 cm. Meanwhile cut the *eringii* into slices about 5 mm thick, and grill the pieces for 2-3 minutes without any oil on the teppan griddle, turning once [5].

4 Arrange the fish and spring onions on 4 serving plates. Pour the sauce around the fish, and garnish on top with fish roe and *eringii* [6]. Serve with a little *wasabi* to one side and garnish with finely shredded leek.

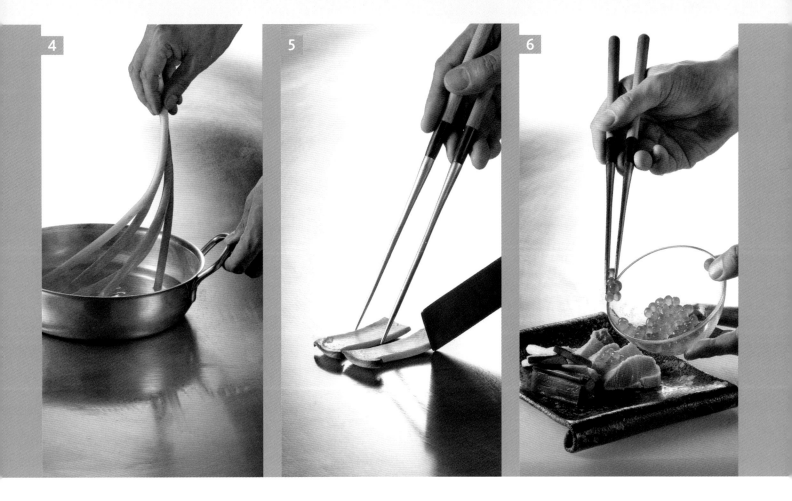

Giant prawns with black vinegar sauce

- 80 g frisée lettuce {1
- 8 pieces of baby corn {2
- 8 leaves of Cos lettuce {3
- 8 sugar snaps {4
- 8 giant prawns
  (about 70 g each) {5
- 125 g flour

> **For the black vinegar sauce**
- 40 ml *kurozu* (black rice vinegar)
- 20 g sugar
- 120 g mayonnaise

before you start

Blanch the baby corn and sugar snaps by dropping them briefly into boiling water, then plunging them into iced water. Allow to cool, then drain and pat dry.

tip

When dusting the prawn with flour, dip just the sides very lightly in a plate of flour, keeping the head and tip of the tail free.

WINE: Tropical fruit (mango, papaya), soft acidity, light oak style.
EXAMPLE: Chardonnay, Bonterra, Mendocino, California USA.

method

1 To make the black vinegar sauce, mix the *kurozu* and sugar well. Add the mayonnaise, and blend thoroughly by hand.

2 Wash the Cos and frisée lettuce. Drain well, and wrap the leaves in a clean tea towel.

3 Shell and de-vein the prawns. Dust them lightly with flour [1].

4 Fry the prawns in a shallow pool of oil on a teppan griddle, at high heat [2]. Cook them very briefly (about 1 minute) on each side, until the surface is crisp. Remove the heads [3], the hard parts of the heads and put to one side [4]. Cut the prawns along the full length of the back. Open them out, turn over and cook further, to cook the inside.

5 Grill the baby corn and sugar snaps very briefly on the teppan griddle, just to warm them up [5].

6 Place the Cos lettuce leaves on individual plates. Position the prawns on the leaves, with the baby corn (cut diagonally in two) on top, then the frisée lettuce and sugar snaps. Pour plenty of sauce over each, and garnish with the prawn heads [6].

Steamed sea bream in a
sea salt case with leek sauce

- 4 trimmed fillets of sea bream, with skins (about 70 g each) {1
- pieces of *konbu* seaweed, {2 4 roughly the same size as the fillets, 4 slightly larger. (*Konbu* left over from a *dashi* stockpot is ideal.)

> For the salt case
- 240 ml egg white
- 1 kg salt
- 120 g *katakuriko* (potato starch)

> For the sauce
- 120 g leek {3
- 100 ml peanut oil
- 3 g salt

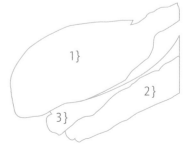

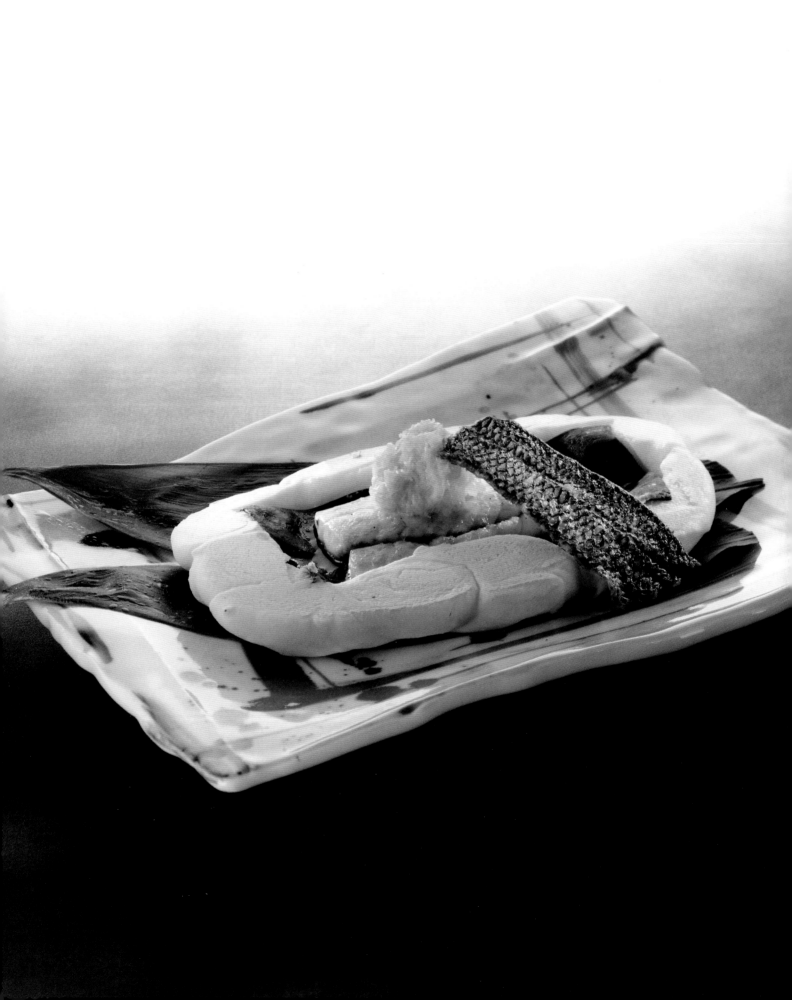

tip

Use a toothpick to keep the seaweed and fish together while cooking.

WINE: Mild, vinous, with green herbs and mineral notes.
EXAMPLE: Saumur Vieilles Vignes, Château Langlois, Loire, France

method

1 To make the salt case, mix the salt and *katakuriko* in a bowl, add the egg whites and beat well until the mixture is firm and forms peaks.

2 To make the sauce, flatten out the central part of the leek, shred it lengthways and then chop finely sideways. Combine the chopped leak with the peanut oil in a pan to make a thick sauce [1A]. Place on the teppan griddle at low heat, stirring frequently and taking care it does not burn [1B]. As the flavours and aromas begin to be released, remove from the heat and mix in the salt. Keep the sauce at room temperature.

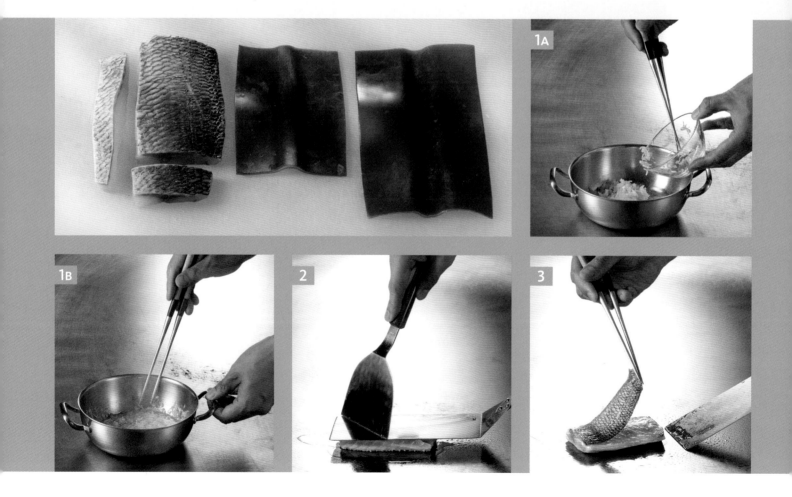

3 Place sea bream fillets skin-side down on the teppan griddle, at high heat for about 30 seconds. Push down firmly on each fillet with a spatula [2], then season lightly with salt and pepper. Turn the fillets over and remove the skins (they should come off easily if the fillets are cooking properly) [3]. Place the skins with the insides downwards on a medium-hot part of the teppan griddle. When they are crisp, remove them from direct heat, but keep warm, and season with salt.

4 Place the smaller pieces of *konbu* on a medium-hot part of the teppan griddle. Put a fillet on each [4A], and cover the fish with the larger *konbu* pieces [4B]. Spoon the salt casing over each portion to cover with a small mound [5]. After a minute, or when the case has hardened and is easy to move, transfer the mounds to a hotter part of the teppan griddle [6]. Leave to steam under a steel cloche for 4 minutes. Remove the cloche, and allow them to steam for a further 6 minutes under the salt casings.

5 Remove the salt casings from the heat, turn them over and remove the outer layer of *konbu* [7].

6 Place fish-side up on individual serving plates. Pile leek paste over each serving, and garnish with the crispy fish skins [8].

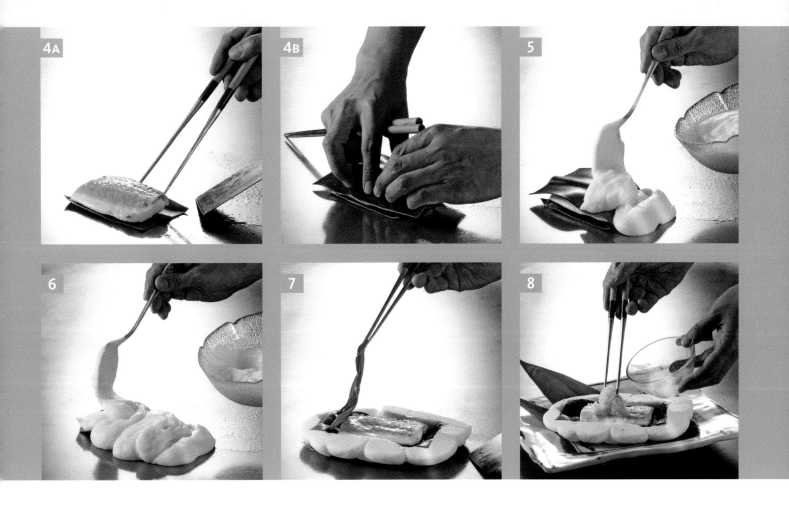

Steamed brill with herbs and ankake wakame sauce

 • 4 brill fillets (80 g each) {1
• 16 g chives {2
• 4 fresh *shiso* leaves {3
• 1 large onion {4

> **For the *ankake wakame* sauce**
• 200 ml *dashi*
• 20 ml *mirin*
• 10 ml light soy sauce
• 2 g dried *wakame* seaweed
• 8 g *katakuriko* (potato starch)
• 10 ml water

• ½ a leek (about 6 cm), finely shredded for garnish {5

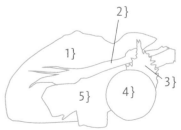

method

1 To make the *ankake wakame* sauce, combine the *dashi*, *mirin* and light soy sauce in a small pot, and bring it to the boil. Dissolve the *katakuriko* in the water. Remove the sauce from the heat, and thicken it by slowly adding the dissolved *katakuriko* [1], stirring constantly. Allow it to simmer for a further 5 minutes. Crumble in the *wakame* [2] and stir through. Keep the sauce warm.

2 Peel the onion, remove the ends, and cut the body into 4 large slices, about 1 cm thick. Smooth a little oil on the teppan griddle, and grill the onion slices over medium heat on just one side, until that side begins to brown. Turn the onions over [3].

WINE: Fresh, youthful, fruity with a mild aftertaste.
EXAMPLE: Pouilly-Fuissé, Domaine Corsin, France

3 Meanwhile, place the brill skin-side up on the oiled teppan griddle, at high heat [4]. Season lightly with salt and pepper, and after a few seconds cut each of the 4 fillets in half. Turn the fillets over, and place one (skin-side down) on each onion ring. Place the other over the first, to give the dish height.

4 Divide the chives and finely shredded leek and *shiso* leaves evenly across all 4 portions, arranging them on top of the fish [5]. Cover with a steel cloche, squirt a little water under the cloche [6], and steam the fish for 3 minutes. The fish is done when a chopstick pokes easily into it.

5 Position the fish on individual plates, and pour *ankake wakame* sauce around each serving.

Lobster with mussels in their shells

- 2 fresh lobsters {1
- 20-28 mussels in shells {2
- 1 stick of celery, with leaves {3
- 1 large onion (60 g) {4
- 10 cm of leek {5
- *miso* chilli sauce (see Sauces)

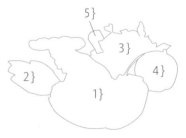

tip

When steaming the lobster with the vegetables and mussels, you will know that the dish is done when first the celery, and then the mussel aromas begin to be released.

WINE: Intense, fine acidity, light confit, plummy fruit, light mineral notes in the final tastes.
EXAMPLE: Chenin Blanc 'Signature', Jean Daniel, Coastal Region of South America.

method

1 Wash whole mussels under running water and set aside. Thinly slice the celery stick (not the leaves) and the onion. Cut the 10 cm piece of leek in 2, then cut the pieces horizontally and separate the layers [1].

2 Cut each lobster in half lengthways. Remove the tomalley (greenish liver in the body cavity) from each half and place on a medium-hot part of the teppan griddle [2]. Leave the tomalleys to grill while the lobsters are cooking, turning just once after about 2 minutes, or when undersides are golden brown.

3 Grill the lobsters shell-side down in small pool of oil at high heat. After about 30 seconds, clean away excess oil around the lobsters, turn them shell-side up [3], and drizzle a little oil over the shells. Cover the lobsters with a metal cloche, squirting a little water under the cloche to steam [4A]. Leave to steam for about 3 minutes.

4 Remove the cloche [4B]. Turn lobsters back onto their shells and remove the flesh from the tails [5]. Chop the flesh into bite-sized pieces [6], and return it to the tails. Return the grilled tomalleys to each half.

5 Place 6-7 mussels in their shells on top of each half lobster [7], then leek and next onion. Finally, layer celery over each [8]. Cover with a cloche and squirt a little water [9] under the cloche to steam. Leave to steam for around 2 minutes, or until the mussels have opened. Remove the cloche [10]. Place each half lobster with its topping in a shallow bowl, and serve with *miso* chilli sauce to the side.

Teppanyaki Restaurant Sazanka and its Chef

Teppanyaki took Masashi Nonaka by surprise. Nonaka-san* graduated from a college of tourism in Japan, and originally wanted to be a tour conductor. Little did he know, when he arrived in Amsterdam in 1985 at the age of 20, that his destiny lay in quite another direction. He was offered a place at the Okura hotel's Teppanyaki Restaurant Sazanka, because he is tall and can bend easily over a teppan griddle. Nonaka-san took to his new role with delight. Ten years later he became sous chef, and in March 2004 he was made Sazanka's chef de cuisine. Now he makes regular trips back to Japan to keep up with the latest trends in teppanyaki cuisine.

In many ways, Chef Nonaka's attraction to the art of teppanyaki is not that far removed from his original desire to be a tour operator. Both involve an enjoyment of interacting with people. Chef Nonaka is inspired by having his guests around him while he cooks. He believes that one of the most essential aspects of teppanyaki cuisine is interpreting guests' reactions and remembering their likes

and dislikes, so that he can tailor each dish to meet an individual's taste — a dash more oil for this person, grill the fish a little longer for that one. Teppanyaki is not 'just cooking', he points out, but an ongoing interaction with the diners. "If you are a chef back in the kitchen, you would need an extraordinarily good waiter out front to pass on such information," he says, "but as a teppan chef you can see it all in people's faces."

Chef Nonaka agrees that part of a teppan chef's role is to entertain, but at Sazanaka you will not find the flamboyant pepper-grinder twirling and knife juggling that has come to characterize teppanyaki in some restaurants around the world. Instead, you are treated to such fine ingredients as *wagyū* beef, delicate lobster and succulent scallops in an atmosphere of poised refinement. A renowned Japanese architectural studio has designed an interior that makes careful use of elemental materials of wood, stone, water and fire to create a particularly Japanese ambience of balance and good taste. Eleven teppan griddles can each

accommodate seven to ten people, and there is a private room for slightly larger gatherings. Chef Nonaka and his team create teppanyaki classics of the very highest calibre, and are constantly coming up with new dishes to titillate adventurous palates.

鉄板焼

さざんか

* Nonaka-san is the Japanese way of saying 'Mr. Nonaka'.

Lightly smoked duck
with duck liver and salad

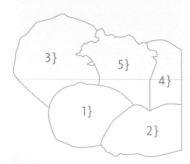

- 160 g duck liver {1
- 2 duck breasts {2

- 4 tablespoons breadcrumbs
- 1 heaped tablespoon of oak chips, mixed with ¾ tablespoon of sugar

> **For the marinade**
- 50 g light *miso*
- 100 g red *miso*
- 50 g sugar
- 25 g honey
- 75 ml sake
- 25 ml *mirin*

> **For the salad**
- 300 g iceberg lettuce {3
- 100 g red-leafed lettuce {4

> **For the soy dressing**
- 4 tablespoons soy sauce
- 3 tablespoons *mirin*
- 2 tablespoons rice vinegar

> **To garnish**
- 4 pieces of *daikon cress* {5
- 2 teaspoons sesame seeds

before you start

Note that the duck has to marinate (see method) for two to three days before cooking.

tip

When cooking the crumbed duck liver, make sure that the breadcrumbs absorb the fat emerging from the liver. This will make the coating crisp and brown.

WINE: Smooth, round in flavour, spicy in the final tastes.
EXAMPLE: Trimbach Gewürztraminer, Ribeauvillé, Alsace, France.

method

1 To make the marinade, combine the light *miso* and the red *miso* with the sugar, honey, sake and *mirin* in a saucepan, and bring to the boil over high heat. Reduce the heat and simmer for 5 minutes, stirring occasionally. Allow to cool completely.

2 Trim the skin off the duck breast. Season the breasts with salt and pepper and cover with cooled marinade [1].Refrigerate for 2 to 3 days before using. Keep the skins refrigerated separately.

3 Just before cooking the duck, shred the iceberg [2] and red lettuces , and place them under cold, running water for 15 minutes. Drain, pat dry with a kitchen towel, and put to one side.

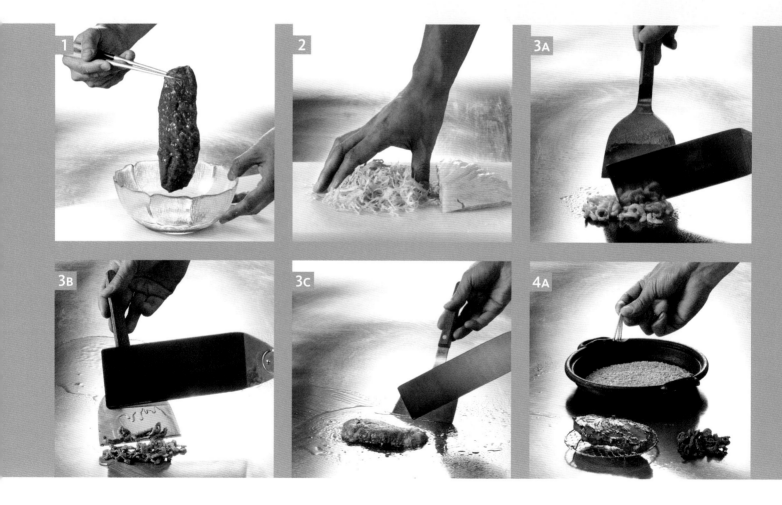

4 Chop the duck skin into small pieces. Grill it on the teppan griddle at high heat [3A], turning frequently until crisp and golden. Put to one side and keep warm [3B]. In the residual duck fat, fry the marinated duck breasts, turning frequently and browning both sides [3C].

5 Place the sugared oak chips in a shallow pan on a teppan griddle at high heat [4A]. When the wood begins to smoke, place the fried duck over it on a grid. Cover and allow to smoke for 6 minutes [4B]. Remove the breasts and slice thinly [4C].

6 Meanwhile, coat the duck liver in breadcrumbs [5A], dice it into cubes of about 1 cm [5B], and grill on a clean, dry part of the teppan griddle.

7 Place the lettuce in 4 bowls. Sprinkle it with sesame seeds and dress it with the soy dressing. Add the sliced duck [6], crumbed duck liver and the crisp-fried skin, and garnish with *daikon cress*.

Fried quail in a soy sauce marinade

- 4 quail fillets {1
- 2 petit onions {2
  (pickling onions)
- 50 g carrot {3
- pinch of dried chilli {4

> For the marinade
- 200 ml *dashi*
- 50 ml soy sauce
- 50 ml *mirin*
- 1 teaspoon sugar
- 3 ½ teaspoons rice vinegar

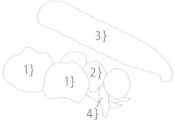

before you start

Make the marinade (see method) some hours before you begin. The quail needs to lie in cooled marinade for at least 1 hour.

tip

Marinated ingredients burn easily on the teppan griddle, so be careful when you are cooking the quail.

WINE: Youthful, light confit, plummy fruit, oak fermented, medium intense.
EXAMPLE: Steen op Hout, Mulderbosch, Stellenbosch, South Africa.

method

1 To make the marinade, cut the onion into thin slices and the carrot into julienne strips. Leave the onion slices to soak in a bowl of water. Before using, drain them and pat dry. Meanwhile, mix the *dashi*, soy sauce, *mirin* and sugar in a saucepan. Bring it to the boil, and remove immediately from the heat. Add the vinegar, carrot, onion, and finally the dried chilli [1]. Set aside to cool.

2 Place the quail fillets in the cooled marinade, and allow to stand for 1 hour.

3 Fry the quail skin-side down in a shallow pool of oil at medium heat, until the skin is crisp [2]. Turn the quail over and continue to cook for about 5 minutes. The fillets will begin to shrink when they are done.

4 Cut the quail fillets into bite-sized portions [3], and divide them between 4 individual serving platters. Pile a little carrot and onion from the marinade alongside [4], and spoon some sauce (at room temperature) over the quail.

Thinly sliced wagyū roll

- 600 g sirloin of *wagyū* beef {1
- 200 g bean sprouts {2
- 120 g spinach {3
- 24 g leek {4
- 4-5 cloves garlic,
  finely chopped {5
- 120 ml garlic-soy sauce
  (see Sauces)

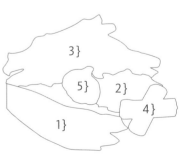

before you start

Cut the *wagyū* into very thin slices. This is most easily done with a meat slicer, when the *wagyū* is frozen. Allow the sliced *wagyū* to thaw. It should stand at room temperature for at least half an hour before you use it.

tip

Make sure to roll the *wagyū* tightly around the leek.

WINE: Round, deep blackberry concentration, smooth, light coffee character, spicy bite in the final tastes.
EXAMPLE: Penfolds Bin 28 Shiraz, Barossa Valley, South Australia.

method

1 Wash, drain and pat dry the spinach and bean sprouts. Toss-fry them together very briefly in a small pool of oil [1], and divide them between 4 serving plates.

2 Fry the finely chopped garlic [2] in a shallow pool of oil at medium heat, until crisp and light-golden brown [3]. Take care not to burn it. Reserve about 4 pinches, and place the rest with the spinach and bean sprouts on the serving plates.

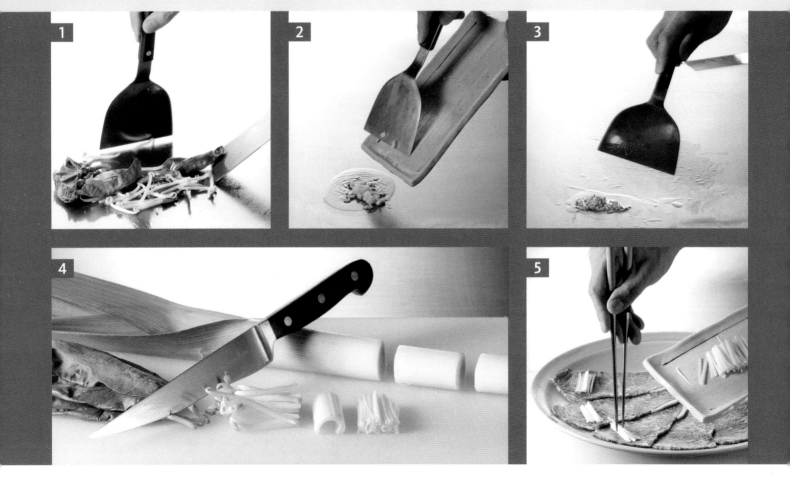

3 Cut the leek lengthways into fine shreds [4]. Place a small pile of the shreds, together with some of the fried garlic, at one end of each piece of *wagyū* [5]. Season lightly with salt and pepper, then roll the beef tightly around the leek, leaving most of the slice unfurled [6].

4 After frying the garlic, mop up excess oil leaving a thin film on the teppan griddle. Grill the part-rolled *wagyū* for a few seconds to seal.

5 Roll up the *wagyū* slices while they are cooking on the plate [7]. Turn once, and as the rolls are cooking, dribble a little garlic-soy sauce down a spatula to season them underneath [8].

6 After a few more seconds, while the *wagyū* is still pink in parts, cut each roll in half [9]. Transfer the pieces to the serving plates.

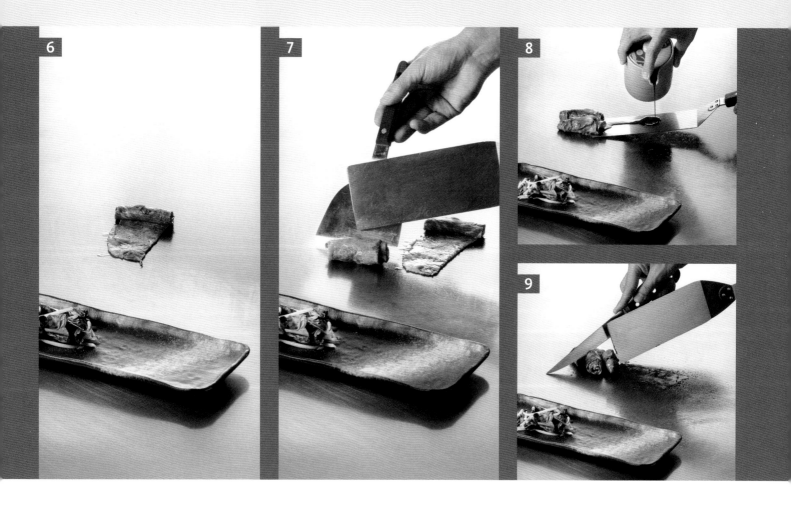

Wagyū steak with vegetables

- 4 *wagyū* sirloin steaks {1
  (200 g each)
- 200 g bean sprouts {2
- 120 g Chinese broccoli {3
- 7 cloves garlic, finely sliced {4

- salt and pepper
- garlic-soy sauce (see Sauces)
- brandy to flambé

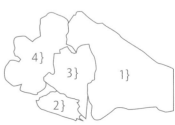

before you start

The *wagyū* steaks should stand at room temperature for at least half an hour before you cook them.

tip

The outside of the *wagyū* steak should have a crisp, char-grilled brown appearance, while the inside should remain pink and juicy.

WINE: Full, smooth, warm spicy hints (cinnamon, cloves), oak fermented, dry wine.
EXAMPLE: Nine Popes, Ch. Milton, Barossa Valley, South Australia.

method

1 Toss-fry the Chinese broccoli and bean sprouts together in a shallow pool of oil on the teppan griddle, at high heat. After a few seconds, move the bean sprouts to a cooler part of the plate. Cover the Chinese broccoli and allow to steam, at medium-high heat [1].

2 Fry the finely sliced garlic in a shallow pool of oil at medium heat [2], until crisp and golden brown [3]. Take care not to burn it. Remove from the oil and keep to one side.

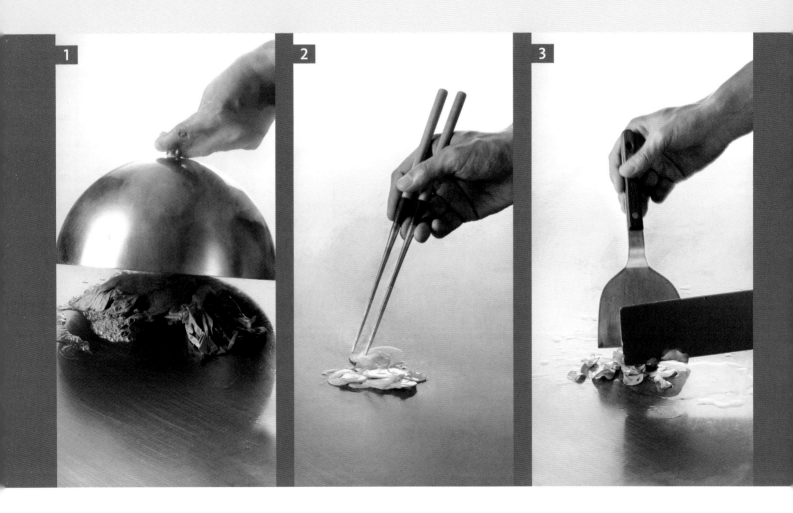

3 Cut off the fatty ends, and chop the fat into tiny cubes (less than 5 mm across) [4], while still on the griddle. Fry them at high heat until crisp [5]. Remove to one side and keep warm. Just before serving, sprinkle the cubes with a little garlic-soy sauce.

4 Fry the *wagyū* steaks at high heat in the remaining oil, searing one side only and seasoning with salt and pepper [6].

5 When the steaks are crisp and brown underneath, turn them over [7]. When both sides are crisp and brown, warm a little brandy in a saucepan and flambé the steaks.

6 Cut the steaks into cubes [8], and serve with the vegetables, crisply fried *wagyū* fat, and garlic alongside.

Terms and Techniques

'Teppan' in Japanese means 'iron plate' and 'yaki' means 'grill', but when a different culture imports a cuisine, it sometimes has to bend its language to accommodate new concepts.

The 'iron plate' on which food is cooked is, in this book, called a teppan griddle. It is sometimes also known as a teppan plate, or teppan pan. Professional teppan griddles not only have a facility for varying their heat level, but are of different temperatures in different parts — the centre is hottest, and the griddle grows cooler towards the edges. This is the reason you will find such instructions in the recipes as: "move to a cooler part of the griddle", or "move to one side of the teppan griddle and keep warm". Of course, if the griddle you are working on is not of variable temperature across its surface, you will need to improvise other ways of, for example, keeping a sauce warm or mixing ingredients off the heat.

The main implements you need for cooking on a teppan griddle are metal spatulas — they come in a variety of shapes and lengths. Sometimes chefs wield two spatulas, one in each hand. Long chopsticks are also useful for delicate work on the griddle (so as not to burn your fingers). As with other branches of Japanese cuisine, an extremely sharp knife is essential.

Unless otherwise stated, the oil used for cooking on the griddle is sunflower oil. Do not use olive oil — it is too volatile, and has too strong a flavour. The griddle should always be oiled lightly before cooking starts.

Broadly speaking, there are three main techniques for cooking on the griddle. Using the terminology employed in this book, they are:

Frying › using a shallow pool of oil on the griddle. You can also fry in oils released by a fatty ingredient (such as duck skin, or fat from the edges of a *wagyū* steak).

Grilling › simply wiping a film of oil over the griddle, and cooking on that. You can also grill having wiped away excess oil or fat after frying something fatty. Some ingredients (especially vegetables) can be grilled without adding oil — though because griddles are oiled before first use, they always have a thin film on them, and grilling is never completely dry.

Steaming › this is often done under a metal cloche. As you cover the item to be steamed, introduce a dash of water under the cloche from a bottle with a dispensing nozzle (of the sort often found on oil and vinegar bottles used for dressing salads at table).

You can also cook sauces and liquids in saucepans directly on the teppan griddle, or smoke ingredients using wood chips in a shallow pan.

It is essential to keep the griddle clean as you cook. This can be done by scraping off charred bits of ingredient with the spatula, and also using the spatula to ladle off excess oil. You can also mop oil off the griddle with a cotton cloth — though it is wise to use the spatula rather than your naked fingers to move the cloth around.

Chef Nonaka advises

➡ *Teppanyaki cooking is far more difficult than it looks! My main advice is practice, practice, practice. The greatest challenge is timing. Time can just shoot by if you are cooking for a number of people. Also, timing is not always constant. With practice you learn to judge for yourself when things are cooked, and to be flexible, so that you can cook something slightly longer for someone who prefers it that way. A good cook is always sensing, feeling — and with practice you can come to respect your own feelings as a cook, to find your own way.*

Renkon mochi
lotus root patties

A recipe from chef Nonaka's mother

- 250 g lotus root {1
- 20 thin slices lotus root

- 3 teaspoons soy sauce
- 2 g salt
- 1 egg {2
- 20 g *katakuriko* (potato starch)

- soy sauce for dipping

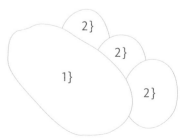

before you start

Make 5 lotus chips per person by placing thinly sliced pieces of lotus root on the teppan griddle at low heat for around an hour, or until crispy rather than chewy. (You can also bake the chips in a low oven.)

tip

Japanese people prefer *renkon mochi* to have a chewy, slightly sticky texture. Test one before serving. If it is not done to your taste, cut the remaining patties in half and cook a little longer.

WINE: Round smooth wine, light spicy, melon and pear fruit, slight yet pleasant bitter flavour in the final tastes.

EXAMPLE: Pinot Blanc Auxerrois, Schoffit, Colmar, France.

method

1 Dice 50 g of peeled lotus root into cubes around 6 mm thick. Place the cubes in boiling water for 2 minutes. Drain well, and allow them to cool.

2 Grate 200 g of peeled lotus root [1], gently draining off excess liquid.

3 Combine the boiled and grated lotus root with three teaspoons soy sauce, the egg, salt and *katakuriko*, and mix well [2]. With a dessert spoon, make ball-shaped patties from the mixture on the teppan griddle [3].

4 Place lotus patties on the teppan griddle at medium heat. Turn after a few minutes, as the underside begins to brown. You can tell the patties are cooked when they are springy to the touch [4].

5 Serve garnished with the lotus chips, and with a little soy sauce to one side for dipping.

Mixed mushrooms steamed in aluminium foil

- 100 g oyster mushrooms { 1
- 80 g *honshimeji* mushrooms { 2
- 70 g *shiitake* mushrooms { 3
- 70 g *enoki* mushrooms { 4
- 100 g *eringii* mushrooms { 5

- 8 g *yuzu* rind, cut into fine filaments { 6
- 280 ml *konbu dashi*

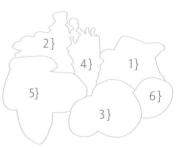

tip

Once the folded foil pouch is cooking on the teppan griddle, press the seams firmly with your spatula to provide an extra-tight seal.

WINE: Light, ripe fruit (plums, cherries), fine acidity, medium bodied, warm spicy aftertaste (cloves, cinnamon).
EXAMPLE: Cims de Porrera, Solanes, Priorat, Spain

method

1 Cut the mushrooms into bite-sized pieces, but not too small. The oyster mushrooms and *shiitake* (stalks removed) are best sliced in 3 across the crowns. With the *honshimeji* and *enoki*, remove the thick base then separate individual stems. Trim the base off the *eringii*, then cut them lengthways into 2 or 3 pieces [1].

2 Take a piece of cooking foil 30cm x 30cm. Bunch the mushrooms in the middle of the foil, keeping the *eringii* and *honshimeji* on the bottom, then the oyster mushrooms and *shiitake*, with the *enoki* on top. Season with salt and pepper.

3 Pour the dashi over the mushrooms [2], and place the filaments of *yuzu* on top.

4 Carefully fold the foil into a pouch — first one end to the other, making a tight seam with the edges, then closing the 2 remaining sides. Ensure the seams are airtight by folding them a number of times, and pressing down firmly.

5 Place the foil pouch on a medium-hot teppan griddle. After it balloons up [3], move it to medium-low heat. Allow around 5 minutes for the mushrooms to steam in the foil balloon. (If, in the end, they are not done to your taste, you can always return the open pouch to the teppan griddle to simmer them a little longer.)

6 Remove the pouch to a low heat side. Pierce it, open out the foil [4] and serve immediately.

Fried tofu with ankake sauce

- 400 g firm tofu, drained and dried {1
- 1 red paprika {2
- 1 green paprika {3
- 1 yellow paprika {4
- ¼ courgette {5

> **For the *ankake* sauce**
- 330 ml *konbu dashi*
- 24 ml light soy sauce
- 10 g sugar
- 2 g *yuzu* peel {6
- 15 g *katakuriko* (potato starch), plus a little extra for coating tofu
- 3 teaspoons water

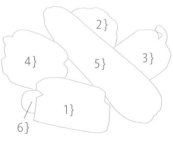

tip

Ankake sauce is very versatile, so feel free to substitute other vegetables for paprika and courgette if you wish.

WINE: Fresh acidity, light confit, tropical fruit, dry mineral aftertaste.
EXAMPLE: Riesling Spätlese, Ürziger Wurzgarten, Merkelbach, Mosel Saar Ruwer, Germany.

method

1 To make the *ankake* sauce, combine the *dashi*, soy sauce and sugar in a saucepan, and bring to the boil. Add the finely cut *yuzu* rind. Dissolve the *katakuriko* in the water. Once the *dashi* mixture has boiled, remove it from the heat and carefully add the dissolved *katakuriko* to thicken the sauce, stirring constantly. Allow to simmer for a further 5 minutes, then set aside.

2 Top-and-tail the paprika, then make a julienne of the sides, cutting them into strips about 5 mm x 3 cm. Cut the unpeeled courgette in half and hollow it out, leaving a centimetre or so of flesh attached to the rind. Slice this outer part of the courgette to make green-and-white julienne strips [1].

3 Grill the sliced vegetables for a few seconds on a thin film of oil, at high heat on the teppan griddle, tossing them all the time with 2 spatulas [2]. When the vegetables begin to soften, remove and add them to the sauce [3].

4 Dust the piece of tofu with *katakuriko* [4]. (Do this just before cooking, or the tofu will dry out.) Fry it in a shallow pool of oil, with the teppan griddle at high heat. Rotate the tofu on the teppan griddle, allowing a minute or so for each edge, or until each surface starts to brown [5]. Scrape up excess oil from the teppan griddle, and dribble it over the tofu as it cooks.

5 Slice the cooked tofu while it is on the pan. Steady the tofu with your spatula, and use a very sharp knife and decisive strokes [6]. (This takes some practice. You may find it easier to slice the tofu earlier, and cook the pieces individually.)

6 Transfer the sliced tofu to a plate, pour the *ankake* sauce with vegetables over it [7], and serve immediately.

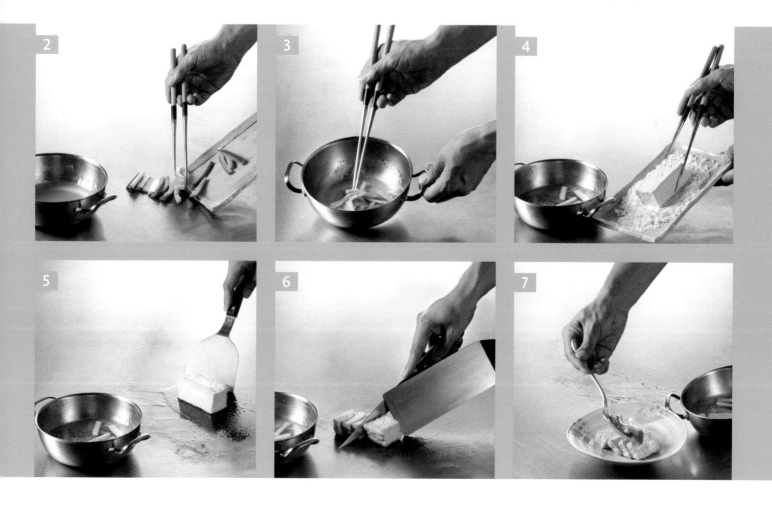

Yakimeshi fried rice

- 200 g chicken leg (drumstick, deboned) {1
- 50 g onion {2
- 40 g carrot {3
- 30 g *naganegi* or spring onion {4
- 2 eggs {5
- 4 teaspoons garlic-soy sauce (see Sauces)
- 200 g cooked rice (warm) {6

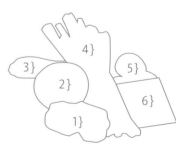

before you start

Finely dice the onion, carrot and *naganegi* onion.
Place the steamed or cooked rice to one side at low heat
on the teppan griddle to keep warm.

tip

When stir-frying the rice, be careful not to crush and
damage the kernels, as this causes it to become sticky.

WINE: Fruity red wine with cherry flavours,
medium body, subtle, soft final tastes.
EXAMPLE: Pinot Noir, Hamilton Russell,
Hemel en Aarde Valley, South Africa.

method

1 Wipe the teppan pan with oil. Sear the chicken briefly
on each side [1]. Remove the skin and dice the chicken
into 1 cm cubes [2].

2 Stir-fry the chicken cubes in a small amount of oil [3].
Add the onion and carrot [4], and stir-fry a little
more. Put the mixture to one side on the teppan griddle,
at low heat to keep warm.

3 Put a little more oil on the teppan griddle [5], at
high heat. When the oil warms up, pour the eggs
onto it [6]. Toss and turn quickly, keeping the eggs quite
raw and oily.

4 When the egg is still only half cooked [7], place it on top of the rice [8]. Mop up the excess oil. Return the rice and egg to the hot part of the teppan griddle and stir-fry for 3 minutes, tossing gently [9].

5 If the chicken cubes and vegetables have been sweating, stir-fry them separately for a few seconds to dry them out, then add them to the rice. Combine thoroughly, and stir-fry for another 2 minutes [10].

6 Season with salt and pepper, make a hollow in the center of the pile and add the *naganegi* [11]. Move the rice to a cooler part of the teppan griddle (at medium to low heat). Sprinkle in garlic-soy sauce [12], and wait for it to warm up. Mix the sauce into the rice, and stir-fry until dry .

Yakisoba
fried noodles

- 600 g Chinese wheat noodles {1 (steamed)
- 160 g cabbage {2
- 40 g carrot {3
- 120 g bean sprouts {4
- 100 g thinly sliced beef {5
- 4 small prawns (around 30 g each) {6
- 120 g squid {7

> **For the *yakisoba* sauce**
- 48 ml *chuuno* sauce
- 48 ml Worcestershire sauce
- 3 teaspoons soy sauce

> **To garnish**
- 20 g *beni shōga* (Japanese pickle)
- 4 teaspoons *aonori* (powdered seaweed)

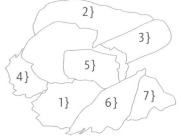

before you start

Make the *yakisoba* sauce, simply by combining the *chuuno*, Worcestershire and soy sauces.

tip

After adding the noodles, lift all the ingredients from the griddle to allow air to enter underneath. This helps cook the noodles.

WINE: Full, exotic wine (papaya, carambola flavours), medium acidity, smooth, light, toasty, oak fermented.
EXAMPLE: Chardonnay 'Max-Reserva', Errázuriz, Casablanca Valley, Chile.

method

1 Wash, drain and dry the vegetables and sprouts. Slice the cabbage into strips 1 cm wide. Make a julienne of the carrots [1]. Also cut the beef into 1 cm thin strips.

2 Fry the prawns and squid in a small pool of oil, with the teppan griddle at high heat. After a few seconds, cut them into bite-sized portions [2].

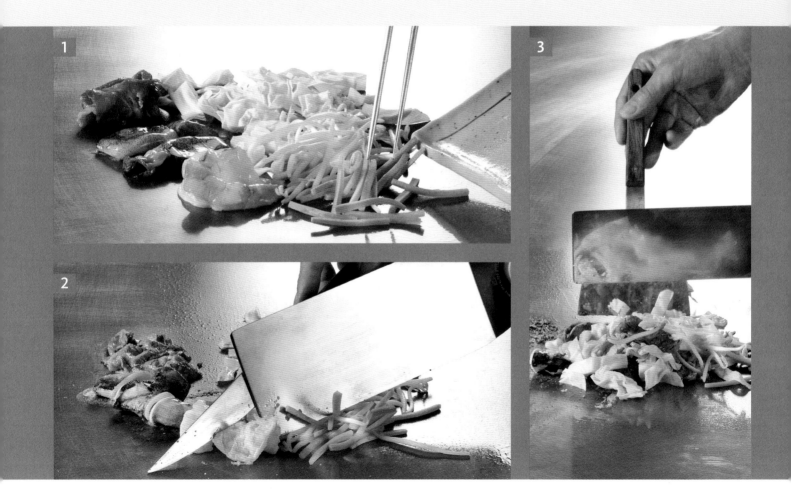

3 Add the beef, carrots, cabbage and sprouts and stir-fry briefly [3].

4 Place the noodles on top of the other ingredients, and season with salt and pepper. Lift all the ingredients from the griddle for a moment to allow air to enter the mix [4]. Leave to cook on the griddle for a minute, then stir-fry briefly.

5 Move the *yakisoba* aside, to a part of the teppan griddle at medium heat. Add the *yakisoba* sauce [5], wait for a few seconds for it to warm up, then mix it in and briefly stir-fry.

6 Serve with a sprinkle of *aonori* powder, and *beni shōga* as garnish to one side [6].

Okonomiyaki

- 90 ml *dashi*
- 60 g flour
- 1 egg

- 4 large prawns {1 (about 16 cm long)
- 120 g squid {2
- 4 scallops {3 (about 30 g each)
- 160 g cabbage {4

- 24 g mayonnaise
- 20 g *beni shōga* (Japanese pickle)
- 16 g dry bonito flakes
- *sōsu* (thick Japanese Worcester Sauce)

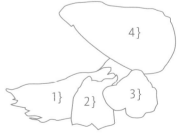

tip

When cooking the *okonomiyaki* on the teppan griddle, touch it very lightly with the spatula to shape it — do not push it down too firmly. If compressed, it takes longer to cook.

method

1 To make the *okonomiyaki* batter, mix the flour and *dashi* in a bowl, add the egg and beat well.

2 Shred the cabbage, and add the batter mixture spoon by spoon [1] to the cabbage, turning it through until the mixture resembles a thick coleslaw.

WINE: Fine acidity, lightly developed white fruit, slightly oak-fermented and mineral notes in the final tastes.
EXAMPLE: Verdejo Belondrade Y Lurton,
Bodegas Lurton, Rueda, Spain.

3 Add the squid, prawns and scallops, cut into bite-sized portions and mix them with the coleslaw [2].

4 Place the mixture in 4 equal mounds on a teppan griddle wiped with oil, at low heat [3]. Flatten very gently, and grill for 3 minutes. Flip each *okonomiyaki* over carefully [4], keeping it in one piece, and cook for a further 5 minutes. Flip once more, then remove to serving plates [5].

5 Spread *sōsu* over the *okonomiyaki* like honey on bread [6]. Zigzag mayonnaise over the top [7], and sprinkle with bonito flakes [8]. Garnish to one side with *beni shōga*.

Sauces

TERIYAKI SAUCE

SOY VINAIGRETTE

UMEBOSHI SAUCE

LEMON BUTTER SAUCE

PICKLES RÉMOULADE

WASABI RÉMOULADE

RED MISO SAUCE

RASPBERRY SAUCE

NORI SEAWEED SAUCE

GREEN PEPPER SAUCE

SAUCE RAVIGOTE

LEEK SAUCE

SALAD DRESSING

GARLIC-SOY SAUCE

SESAME SAUCE

MISO PEANUT SAUCE

MISO CHILLI SAUCE

soy sauce	200 ml
mirin	150 ml
rice vinegar	100 ml

method — Simply mix all the ingredients together in a bowl.

soy sauce	700 ml
mirin	200 ml
garlic	120 g
ginger	20 g

method — Mash the garlic and ginger into a thick mixed paste. Add the soy sauce and the *mirin*, and stir well. Leave the mixture to stand at room temperature for at least 3 weeks, stirring twice a week, for it to reach optimum flavour. Only small amounts are needed for the recipes in this book, but the sauce may be kept for 6 months.

red *miso*	250 g
mirin	250 ml
dashi	500 ml
sugar	50 g
puréed sesame seed	250 g
sesame seeds	50 g

method — Mix all ingredients except the sesame seeds in a saucepan. Bring the mixture to the boil, then remove from heat and allow to cool. Toast the sesame seeds in a pan for a minute or 2, then mix them into the sauce.

red *miso*	250 g
mirin	250 ml
dashi	450 ml
sugar	20 g
peanut butter	100 g

method — Simply mix all the ingredients well together.

red *miso*	200 g
white *miso*	50 g
tomato purée	100 g
mirin	150 ml
water	180 ml
sesame oil	75 ml
sambal	4 g

method — Mix all the ingredients except sesame oil and *sambal* in a saucepan, and bring to the boil. Remove the mixture from the heat, and allow to cool. When cool, mix in the sesame oil and the *sambal*. If you prefer the sauce spicy, you can add some more *sambal* or powdered chilli.

Crêpes with berries and ice cream

- 64 g blueberries {1
- 40 g red currants {2
- 100 g blackberries {3
- 20 g raspberries {4
- 48 g cape gooseberries {5

> For the marinade
- 100 ml water
- 2 tablespoons sugar
- 2 ½ teaspoons white wine

> For the crêpes
- 250 g plain flour
- 4 eggs
- 750 ml milk
- 45 g butter

This is sufficient for 20 crêpes.
The remainder may be frozen
for future use.

- 4 scoops vanilla ice cream
- 120 ml chocolate sauce
- Grand Marnier liqueur

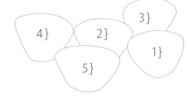

before you start

The fruit will need to marinate (see method) for at least 2 to 3 days before you make the dessert.

tip

Keep the crêpe really thin, otherwise it will overwhelm the other flavours.

WINE: Light blueberry taste, fine acidity, light confit in the final tastes.
EXAMPLE: Zweigelt Beerenauslese, A.Kracher, Neusiedlersee, Austria.

method

1 Combine the sugar and water in a saucepan and bring to the boil over high heat, stirring occasionally. Add the wine, and allow to cool completely. Place all the fruit in a bowl, and cover it with the marinade. Cover the bowl and refrigerate for at least 2-3 days.

2 To make the crêpes, beat the eggs until smooth, then add the milk. Sift the flour into a small bowl, and gradually add the egg mixture. Heat up the butter, add it to the mixture, and whisk to make a smooth batter.

3 Grease the teppan griddle with oil. For each crêpe, spoon a small soup ladle of the batter onto the griddle [1A], and cook at medium heat [1B]. Flip when the underside is light brown [2].

4 Place portions of marinated berries on 4 serving platters [3]. Position a scoop of ice cream in the centre of each crêpe [4], and add a little of the chocolate sauce. Roll up the crêpes [5], and place one on top of each serving of berries [6].

5 Decorate each dessert with the rest of the chocolate sauce [7]. Warm a little Grand Marnier liqueur in a small saucepan, then set it alight, pour over crêpes to flambé and serve [8].

Strawberries and blueberries in a timbale with ice cream

- 12 strawberries, chopped {1
- 48 g blueberries {2

> **For the strawberry *coulis*** {3
- 100 g strawberries
- 25 g sugar
- 2 ½ teaspoons lemon juice
- 1 teaspoon strawberry liqueur

> **For the timbales**
- 100 g melted butter
- 100 g powdered sugar
- 100 g egg white
- 100 g plain flour

This makes more than you will need for 4 timbales. Additional timbales may be frozen for future use.

- 4 scoops of ice cream
- mint to garnish {4
- Kirsch liqueur

before you start

The strawberries for the *coulis* need to marinate overnight (see method), before you make the dessert.

WINE: Fresh apple acidity, tropical fruit (passion fruit), light confit to the final tastes.
EXAMPLE: Sauvignon Blanc Late Harvest, Errázuriz, Casablanca Valley, Chile

method

1 To make the *coulis*, dice 100 g strawberries into 5 mm pieces. Mix in the sugar and lemon juice (together with the juices released by the strawberries), and marinate in a jar for 24 hours. Next day, separate out the strawberries. Heat the remaining liquid to boiling, and allow to cool. Mash the strawberries or pulp them in a blender. Add 18 ml of the liquid to the strawberry pulp and mix well. Finally, add the strawberry liqueur.

2 To make the timbales, place melted butter in a bowl and add powdered sugar, a little at a time (in 3 separate additions) mixing constantly. Gradually add the egg white, also bit by bit, and finally the flour, mixing each in well. Spoon 4 portions of about 1 tablespoon each onto 4 circles of silicone paper. Cover each with another piece of silicone paper, and flatten them by hand.

3 Grill the paper-covered timbale dough on both sides, on a teppan griddle with no oil, at medium heat. Press flat with a spatula while cooking [1]. After about 2 minutes, when the timbales are ready, the silicone paper will begin to peel off. Remove it [2], and continue to grill the dough circles, flipping frequently, until they are golden brown.

4 Remove the dough circles from the heat, and mould them into timbale shapes between two ramekins [3].

5 Combine the blueberries and chopped strawberries in a bowl and place a little of the mixture in each timbale [4]. Coat with strawberry *coulis* [5].

6 Warm some Kirsch liqueur in a saucepan, and light it to flambé the ice cream. Add a scoop of the flambéed ice cream to each timbale. Garnish each serving with mint [6] and powdered sugar, and serve.

Matcha dorayaki

> **For the custard pumpkin cream**

- 5 g plain flour
- 13 g sugar
- half an egg yoke
- 50 ml milk
- 100 g pumpkin paste {1

> **For the *matcha dorayaki* dough**

- 65 g plain flour
- 24 g baking powder
- 20 g rice flour
- 8 g *matcha* (powdered green tea)
- 40 g sugar
- 2 eggs
- 1 tablespoon fresh cream
- 3 tablespoons sunflower oil

Fruit in season {2 {3

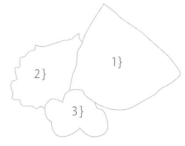

tip

WINE: Light yellow, plummy, hints of honey, medium intensity to the round soft final aftertaste.
EXAMPLE: Jurançon 'Ballet d'Octobre', Cauhapé, France.

method

1 To make the custard cream, whip the egg yolk with sugar then add the flour. Place in a *bain-marie* on the teppan griddle, and add the milk little by little, stirring constantly until thickened. Allow to cool completely, then stir in the pumpkin paste.

2 To make the *matcha dorayaki* dough, combine the flour and baking powder with the rice flour, *matcha* and sugar in a bowl. Add the eggs, fresh cream and lastly the oil, and mix well.

3 Wipe the teppan griddle with oil. Spoon equal amounts of the *matcha doryaki* dough onto the griddle [1] to make 4 circular pancakes, about 1 cm high. Grill at medium-low heat for about 3 minutes, taking care not to burn. Turn the *matcha dorayaki* once to cook the other side, for 2 minutes [2].

4 Next, spread each of the *matcha dorayaki* with the custard cream [3], and fold them in half [4A-B]. Cut the *matcha dorayaki* into 2 pieces [5], and serve with seasonal fruit, such as cherries or sliced pitahaya.

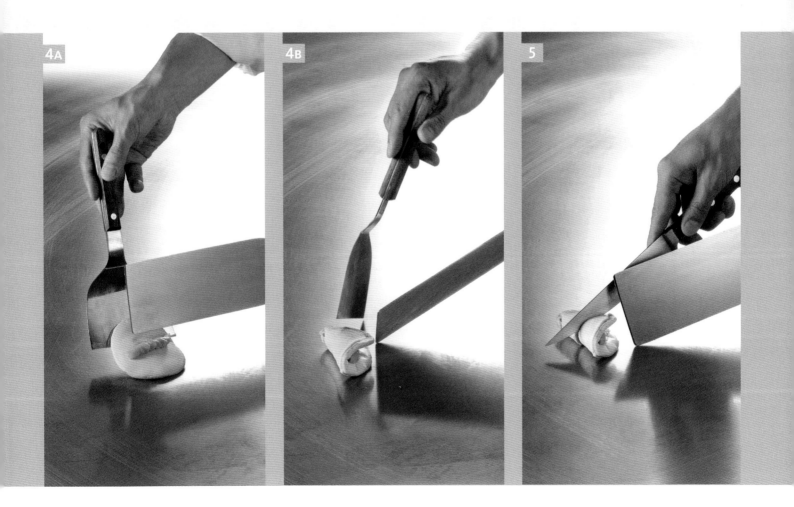

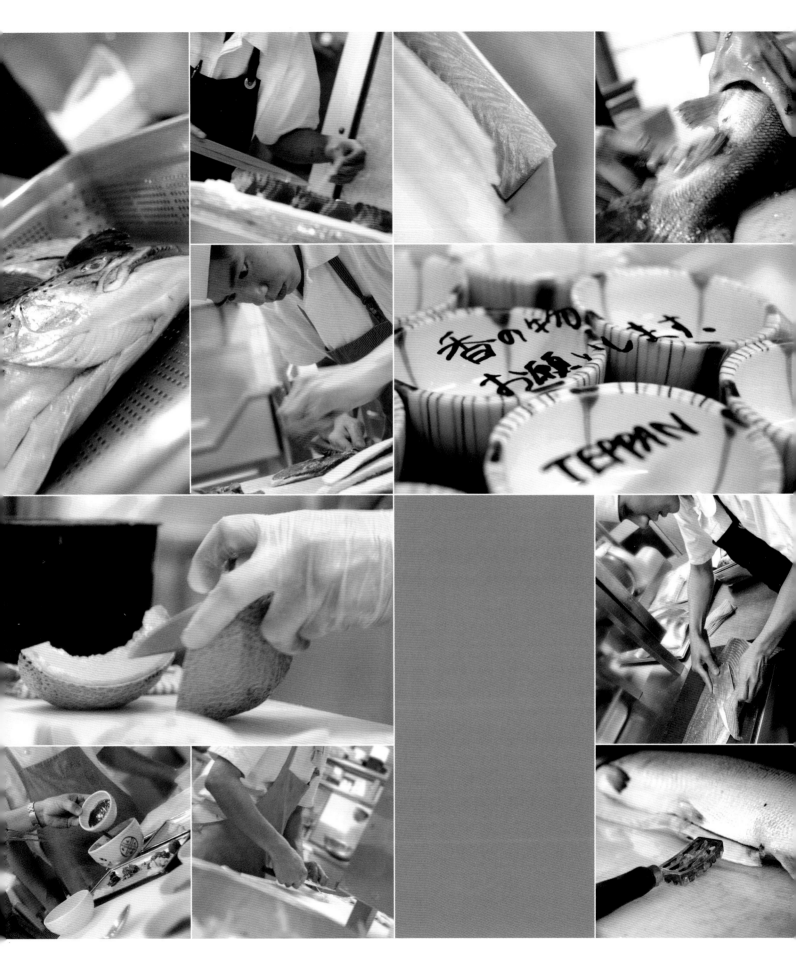

Ingredients

A guide to some of the less familiar ingredients in the recipes, and a few possible substitutes.

AONORI — spice made from dried edible green seaweed, sold flaked.

BENI SHOGA — Japanese pickle, made with ginger and red *shiso*.

CHINESE BROCCOLI — called *kai-lan* in Chinese. A leafy vegetable with a similar taste to broccoli, but a little more bitter.

CHUUNO — a Japanese commercially bottled sauce, similar to Worcestershire Sauce, but thicker, fruitier and sweeter.

DAIKON CRESS — cress of the Japanese giant white radish. Daikon cress is a very popular item in Japan, produced from local radish seeds, with the flavour of horseradish.

DASHI — the all-purpose Japanese stock. The basic *dashi* is made with bonito flakes and *konbu* (giant kelp). Unless otherwise specified, this is what is meant by *dashi* in the recipes in this book, though the vegetarian dishes require *dashi* made

from *konbu* alone. You can make your own stock, but instant, powdered *dashi* is available.

KATAKURIKO — potato starch, used for thickening sauces. Originally, *katakuriko* meant a starch extracted from the bulb of the dog-tooth violet, but has now come to refer generically to the far cheaper potato starch.
Substitute: Cornstarch may be substituted, but you will need to use a little more, as *katakuriko* is stronger.

KUROSU — 'black vinegar', an aged vinegar made from unpolished rice, and sometimes barley.

MATCHA — powdered green tea leaves, made from the finest young leaves on the bush.

MIRIN — a sweet liquid flavouring, made by fermenting glutinous rice with distilled spirits.

MISO — fermented soya bean paste. It comes in many different

types. In addition to basic *miso*, those used here are 'red *miso*' (savoury, made with barley added) and 'light *miso*' (sweeter, injected with rice mould).

NAGANEGI — also known as Japanese long onion. Spring onions make a reasonable substitute.

SHISO — a member of the mint family, sometimes called *'perilla'* (for green varieties) or 'beefsteak plant' (for red ones) in English. Green *shiso* is used mainly as an edible garnish, and red *shiso* in pickling.

SOSU — a thick commercial bottled sauce, also known as Japanese Worcestershire Sauce

SOY SAUCE — Japanese soy sauce is generally thinner, sweeter and less salty than Chinese soy sauce. It is graded into light and dark soy sauce. Though clearer and thinner than dark soy sauce, light soy sauce is saltier. Dark soy sauce has more body.

WAGYU — generally known as *wagyū* beef, a supremely flavoursome, intensely marbled beef. For more information, see www.nicetomeat.nl

WAKAME SEAWEED — a member of the algae family, usually sold dried.

YUZU — Japanese citron. The rind, either fresh or dried, is used for its zesty aroma.
Substitute: Lime or lemon zest make a reasonable substitute, or you might use *yuzu* juice.

Special Thanks to

Yuji Matsuda (Sous-chef Sazanka Restaurant)

Kuniyoshi Ohtawara (Teppancook Sazanka Restaurant)

Noël Vanwittenbergh (Sommelier)

Nicole Pauptit (Co-ordinator)

Text

Rodney Bolt

Masashi Nonaka (recipes)

Kasia Cwiertka (introduction)

Photography

Stephane Verheye and Olivier Chenoix

Final editing

Hilde Deweer

Layout and Printing

Group Van Damme bvba, Oostkamp (B)

Published by

Stichting Kunstboek

Legeweg 165

B – 8020 Oostkamp

T. +32 (0)50 46 19 10

F. +32 (0)50 46 19 18

info@stichtingkunstboek.com

www.stichtingkunstboek.com

ISBN 978-90-5856-298-2

D/2008/6407/36

NUR 441